W9-CUB-725

INNER REFLECTIONS

Engagement Calendar 2021

SELECTIONS FROM THE WRITINGS OF
PARAMAHANSA YOGANANDA

SELF-REALIZATION FELLOWSHIP

ॐ In Divine Love to Chetana a Blessed year
Your sister Sreemata

COPYRIGHT © 2020 SELF-REALIZATION FELLOWSHIP
All rights reserved.

FRONT COVER:
Gordon Lake, Ontario, Canada
Photograph by Don Johnston
Design by Mir Abu

NOTE: *Holidays and other observed dates are included for the United States (U.S.), Canada, United Kingdom (U.K.), Australia, and New Zealand (N.Z.).*
Moon phases, equinoxes, and solstices are based on Pacific Standard Time (UTC – 8 hours).

No part of this calendar may be reproduced in any form or by any means without written permission from the publisher:
Self-Realization Fellowship, 3880 San Rafael Avenue,
Los Angeles, California 90065-3219, U.S.A.

Printed in Italy
4854-J6272

The scenery of mountains painted on the ever-changing azure canvas of the sky,
the mysterious mechanism of the human body, the rose, the green grass carpet,
the magnanimity of souls, the loftiness of minds,
the depth of love — all these things remind us
of a God who is beautiful and noble.

—Paramahansa Yogananda

~

THE PHOTOGRAPHS IN THIS CALENDAR are accompanied by selections from the writings of Paramahansa Yogananda, whose timeless and universal teachings have awakened many — of all races, cultures, and creeds — to a deeper awareness of the one reality that sustains and unites us all.

Whether spread over the vast heavens or hidden in the exquisite delicacy of a tiny flower, nature's beauty is always beckoning, inviting us to look behind the outward form and sense the presence of God within.

We hope that the thoughts and images in these pages will bring you inspiration and encouragement in the days and weeks of the coming year.

Gordon Lake, Ontario, Canada   Photograph by Don Johnston

Picture the New Year as a garden you are responsible for planting. Sow the seeds of good habits in this soil and weed out worries and wrong actions of the past.

—Paramahansa Yogananda

Spring crocuses   Photograph by Martin Ruegner/Masterfile

December/January

Advaita retreat

Day # 2

28
monday

Full Moon ○ Day #3

29
tuesday

Day #4

30
wednesday

Day #5

31
thursday

Celebrating Silence retreat
3[45] on

New Year's Day

1
friday

Day #2

2
saturday

Day #3

3
sunday

December 2020

S	M	T	W	T	F	S
		1	2	3	4	5
6	7	8	9	10	11	12
13	14	15	16	17	18	19
20	21	22	23	24	25	26
27	28	29	30	31		

January

S	M	T	W	T	F	S
					1	2
3	4	5	6	7	8	9
10	11	12	13	14	15	16
17	18	19	20	21	22	23
24/31	25	26	27	28	29	30

January

4
monday
SF satsang

5
tuesday
Paramahansa Yogananda's Birthday

6
wednesday
Last Quarter ◑

7
thursday

8
friday

9
saturday

10
sunday

January

S	M	T	W	T	F	S
					1	2
3	4	5	6	7	8	9
10	11	12	13	14	15	16
17	18	19	20	21	22	23
24/31	25	26	27	28	29	30

February

S	M	T	W	T	F	S
	1	2	3	4	5	6
7	8	9	10	11	12	13
14	15	16	17	18	19	20
21	22	23	24	25	26	27
28						

I want to hear Thy quiet voice ever singing in the silence of my soul.

—Paramahansa Yogananda

Sunset on the American River, Sacramento, California   Photograph by Lewis Kemper

Every soul has some unique quality that no one else has. Every soul is hallowed because in each one there is an individual expression of the Infinite found in no one else.

—Paramahansa Yogananda

Juvenile golden damselfish, Great Barrier Reef, Australia   Photograph by Gary Bell/Oceanwide Images

January

12-2 PA plumbing (Dustin)

11
monday

3:30 library

12
tuesday

New Moon ●

13
wednesday

14
thursday

15
friday

January

S	M	T	W	T	F	S
					1	2
3	4	5	6	7	8	9
10	11	12	13	14	15	16
17	18	19	20	21	22	23
24/31	25	26	27	28	29	30

February

S	M	T	W	T	F	S
	1	2	3	4	5	6
7	8	9	10	11	12	13
14	15	16	17	18	19	20
21	22	23	24	25	26	27
28						

16
saturday

1 - COVID - vaccine

17
sunday

January

18
monday

1145 Meet

Martin Luther King, Jr.'s Birthday (Observed)

19
tuesday

9 Inaugeration

20
wednesday

4- library

First Quarter ◐

21
thursday

Noon - DrCho

22
friday

23
saturday

24
sunday

January

S	M	T	W	T	F	S
					1	2
3	4	5	6	7	8	9
10	11	12	13	14	15	16
17	18	19	20	21	22	23
24/31	25	26	27	28	29	30

February

S	M	T	W	T	F	S
	1	2	3	4	5	6
7	8	9	10	11	12	13
14	15	16	17	18	19	20
21	22	23	24	25	26	27
28						

In the solitude of my inner silence I have found the paradise of unending Joy.

—Paramahansa Yogananda

Tropical twilight, Virgin Gorda, British Virgin Islands   Photograph by Mary Liz Austin

Do your best, but be objective, nonattached. Pay attention to the studies life places before you. They contain the lessons you must learn.

—Paramahansa Yogananda

Lion cub, Ngorongoro Conservation Area, Tanzania   Photograph by Russ Burden

January

25
monday

Harry's surgery

Australia Day (Australia)

26
tuesday

27
wednesday

925-831-192

11 15 Alice

Full Moon ○

28
thursday

10 30 Aurore

29
friday

JANUARY

S	M	T	W	T	F	S
					1	2
3	4	5	6	7	8	9
10	11	12	13	14	15	16
17	18	19	20	21	22	23
24/31	25	26	27	28	29	30

FEBRUARY

S	M	T	W	T	F	S
	1	2	3	4	5	6
7	8	9	10	11	12	13
14	15	16	17	18	19	20
21	22	23	24	25	26	27
28						

30
saturday

31
sunday

February

1
monday

~~Noon~~ 1^15 - Dr Muller

2
tuesday

3
wednesday

4
thursday

Last Quarter

NP Tam
↓ 1^40

5
friday

6
saturday

7
sunday

FEBRUARY

S	M	T	W	T	F	S
	1	2	3	4	5	6
7	8	9	10	11	12	13
14	15	16	17	18	19	20
21	22	23	24	25	26	27
28						

MARCH

S	M	T	W	T	F	S
	1	2	3	4	5	6
7	8	9	10	11	12	13
14	15	16	17	18	19	20
21	22	23	24	25	26	27
28	29	30	31			

Practice the presence of peace. The more you do that, the more you will feel the presence of that power in your life.

—Paramahansa Yogananda

Daybreak, Harvard Pond, Petersham, Massachusetts   Photograph by Paul Rezendes

When two souls come together and bring out the wholeness in each other and ultimately unite with Spirit, that union is a true marriage between soul mates.

—Paramahansa Yogananda

Calla lilies, Seabeck, Washington   Photograph by Don Paulson

February

11-Dr Lusa

8
monday

9
tuesday

4<u>20</u> Dr. Gaeta
V.V

10
wednesday

11. Jan

New Moon ●

11
thursday

4- Precta

12
friday

FEBRUARY

S	M	T	W	T	F	S
	1	2	3	4	5	6
7	8	9	10	11	12	13
14	15	16	17	18	19	20
21	22	23	24	25	26	27
28						

MARCH

S	M	T	W	T	F	S
	1	2	3	4	5	6
7	8	9	10	11	12	13
14	15	16	17	18	19	20
21	22	23	24	25	26	27
28	29	30	31			

13
saturday

2 Vacc#2

St. Valentine's Day

14
sunday

February

15
monday

Presidents' Day

16
tuesday

17
wednesday

18
thursday

11[15] Alice

2[30] Bob
3[30] Preeta

19
friday

8-1[30] AF

11- ~~Adrianne Tamp~~

4[30] TIA

First Quarter

20
saturday

21
sunday

February

S	M	T	W	T	F	S
	1	2	3	4	5	6
7	8	9	10	11	12	13
14	15	16	17	18	19	20
21	22	23	24	25	26	27
28						

March

S	M	T	W	T	F	S
	1	2	3	4	5	6
7	8	9	10	11	12	13
14	15	16	17	18	19	20
21	22	23	24	25	26	27
28	29	30	31			

As a mirror reflects all things held before it, so when your mind-mirror is calm,
you will be able to see reflected in it the true quality of others.
If you are busy doing good to all, remaining calm and meditative,
the true character of whoever comes to you will be revealed to you.

—Paramahansa Yogananda

Zebras, Maasai Mara National Reserve, Kenya   Photograph by Andre and Anita Gilden/First Light

Whenever you see a beautiful sunset, think to yourself:
"It is God's painting on the sky."

—Paramahansa Yogananda

Indian River Marsh, Titusville, Florida Photograph by Tim Fitzharris

February

~~noon - Arit~~

22
monday

23
tuesday

24
wednesday

1[30] Dr. Adewala
V. V.

25
thursday

26
friday

27
saturday

Full Moon ○

28
sunday

FEBRUARY

S	M	T	W	T	F	S
	1	2	3	4	5	6
7	8	9	10	11	12	13
14	15	16	17	18	19	20
21	22	23	24	25	26	27
28						

MARCH

S	M	T	W	T	F	S
	1	2	3	4	5	6
7	8	9	10	11	12	13
14	15	16	17	18	19	20
21	22	23	24	25	26	27
28	29	30	31			

March

1
monday

2
tuesday

3
wednesday

4
thursday

5
friday

Last Quarter ◑

6
saturday

7
sunday

Paramahansa Yogananda's Mahasamadhi

March

S	M	T	W	T	F	S
	1	2	3	4	5	6
7	8	9	10	11	12	13
14	15	16	17	18	19	20
21	22	23	24	25	26	27
28	29	30	31			

April

S	M	T	W	T	F	S
				1	2	3
4	5	6	7	8	9	10
11	12	13	14	15	16	17
18	19	20	21	22	23	24
25	26	27	28	29	30	

We must learn to simplify the externals of our life
and take time to beautify our inner self.
That is the way to develop true magnetism.

—Paramahansa Yogananda

Golden finch, Southern Illinois   Photograph by Richard & Susan Day

Beyond the gross vibratory boundaries of matter, the Immutable Infinite reigns in all His majesty and vastness....When your soul has expanded and feels its presence everywhere, then you are united with Spirit.

—Paramahansa Yogananda

Lower Antelope Canyon, Arizona   Photograph by Gary Hart

March

8
monday

Sri Yukteswar's Mahasamadhi

9
tuesday

10
wednesday

11
thursday

12
friday

New Moon ●

13
saturday

Daylight Saving Time begins (U.S. and Canada)

14
sunday

MARCH

S	M	T	W	T	F	S
	1	2	3	4	5	6
7	8	9	10	11	12	13
14	15	16	17	18	19	20
21	22	23	24	25	26	27
28	29	30	31			

APRIL

S	M	T	W	T	F	S
				1	2	3
4	5	6	7	8	9	10
11	12	13	14	15	16	17
18	19	20	21	22	23	24
25	26	27	28	29	30	

March

15
monday

11^{45} mint

16
tuesday

2 - Dr Ademola

17
wednesday

St. Patrick's Day

12^{30}

4

1 - Camera

18
thursday

19
friday

20
saturday

Vernal Equinox

21
sunday

First Quarter ◐

MARCH

S	M	T	W	T	F	S
	1	2	3	4	5	6
7	8	9	10	11	12	13
14	15	16	17	18	19	20
21	22	23	24	25	26	27
28	29	30	31			

APRIL

S	M	T	W	T	F	S
				1	2	3
4	5	6	7	8	9	10
11	12	13	14	15	16	17
18	19	20	21	22	23	24
25	26	27	28	29	30	

In each soul is the unique imprint of the grace of God. Nowhere in the world is there another exactly like you.

—Paramahansa Yogananda

Red-spotted purple butterfly Photograph by Darrell Gulin

*D*evelop that consciousness within yourself wherein a little happiness or a little sorrow cannot disturb the calm lake of your mind, for a ruffled mind cannot mirror the reflection of God in the soul.

—Paramahansa Yogananda

Vermillion Lake and Mt. Rundle, Banff National Park, Canada   Photograph by Mike Grandmaison

March

22
monday

11^10 Los Altos Lab appt.

23
tuesday

24
wednesday

9^05

25
thursday

26
friday

March

S	M	T	W	T	F	S
	1	2	3	4	5	6
7	8	9	10	11	12	13
14	15	16	17	18	19	20
21	22	23	24	25	26	27
28	29	30	31			

April

S	M	T	W	T	F	S
				1	2	3
4	5	6	7	8	9	10
11	12	13	14	15	16	17
18	19	20	21	22	23	24
25	26	27	28	29	30	

Passover begins

27
saturday

Daylight Saving Time begins (U.K. and European Union) Full Moon ○

28
sunday

March/April

1-Mariana

29
monday

1-neurology consult
Dr Gershfield
on wait list

30
tuesday

11:15 Tseng Andrea

31
wednesday

10:30 HTGT
11:15 Alice

1
thursday

2
friday

Good Friday

3
saturday

4
sunday

Easter Sunday Last Quarter ◑

March

S	M	T	W	T	F	S
	1	2	3	4	5	6
7	8	9	10	11	12	13
14	15	16	17	18	19	20
21	22	23	24	25	26	27
28	29	30	31			

April

S	M	T	W	T	F	S
				1	2	3
4	5	6	7	8	9	10
11	12	13	14	15	16	17
18	19	20	21	22	23	24
25	26	27	28	29	30	

The duty of friends is to continuously help each other to develop themselves. When souls seek progress together in God, then divine friendship flowers.

—Paramahansa Yogananda

Bald eagles, near Nome, Alaska Photograph by Donna Dewhurst/Accent Alaska

Seek to do brave and lovely things which are left undone by the majority of people. Give gifts of love and peace to those whom others pass by.

—Paramahansa Yogananda

Primroses   Photograph by Raimond Linke/Masterfile

April

11 - Dr. Lisa

Easter Monday (All except U.S. and Scotland)

5
monday

6
tuesday

7
wednesday

8
thursday

9
friday

APRIL

S	M	T	W	T	F	S
				1	2	3
4	5	6	7	8	9	10
11	12	13	14	15	16	17
18	19	20	21	22	23	24
25	26	27	28	29	30	

MAY

S	M	T	W	T	F	S
						1
2	3	4	5	6	7	8
9	10	11	12	13	14	15
16	17	18	19	20	21	22
23/30	24/31	25	26	27	28	29

10
saturday

New Moon ●

11
sunday

April

12
monday

13
tuesday

14
wednesday

15
thursday

16
friday

17
saturday

18
sunday

April

S	M	T	W	T	F	S
				1	2	3
4	5	6	7	8	9	10
11	12	13	14	15	16	17
18	19	20	21	22	23	24
25	26	27	28	29	30	

May

S	M	T	W	T	F	S
						1
2	3	4	5	6	7	8
9	10	11	12	13	14	15
16	17	18	19	20	21	22
23/30	24/31	25	26	27	28	29

God is present behind everything. Him whom I looked for in the clouds
and everywhere, I find in every motion of my body,
and enthroned on the stillness of my mind.

—Paramahansa Yogananda

Torres del Paine National Park, Chile   Photograph by Londie G. Padelsky

Do something that nobody else has done, something that will dazzle the world. Show that God's creative principle works in you.

—Paramahansa Yogananda

Purebred Icelandic horse in lupine field, Iceland   Photograph by B. Mauritius/AGE Fotostock

April

First Quarter ◐

19
monday

20
tuesday

21
wednesday

Earth Day 11[15] Olive

22
thursday

23
friday

April

S	M	T	W	T	F	S
				1	2	3
4	5	6	7	8	9	10
11	12	13	14	15	16	17
18	19	20	21	22	23	24
25	26	27	28	29	30	

May

S	M	T	W	T	F	S
						1
2	3	4	5	6	7	8
9	10	11	12	13	14	15
16	17	18	19	20	21	22
23/30	24/31	25	26	27	28	29

24
saturday

25
sunday

April/May

26
monday

11 - Mariana

Full Moon ○

27
tuesday

28
wednesday

10^{30} - 11^{30} PT GT

29
thursday

30
friday

1
saturday

2
sunday

April						
S	M	T	W	T	F	S
				1	2	3
4	5	6	7	8	9	10
11	12	13	14	15	16	17
18	19	20	21	22	23	24
25	26	27	28	29	30	

May						
S	M	T	W	T	F	S
						1
2	3	4	5	6	7	8
9	10	11	12	13	14	15
16	17	18	19	20	21	22
23/30	24/31	25	26	27	28	29

*U*nderlying all life is the silent voice of God, ever calling to us through flowers, through scriptures, and through our conscience — through all things that are beautiful and that make life worth living.

—Paramahansa Yogananda

Flowering water lily   Photograph by Aflo Relax/Masterfile

The beauty in the world bespeaks the creative motherly instinct of God,
and when we look upon all the good in Nature,
we experience a feeling of tenderness within us.

—Paramahansa Yogananda

Calithea butterfly   Photograph by Darrell Gulin

May

11 · Dr Lisa

Last Quarter ◑

3
monday

2:45 Dr Yamaguchi
3301 Industrial
2nd floor

4
tuesday

5
wednesday

12:30 Aurora

National Day of Prayer

6
thursday

7
friday

MAY

S	M	T	W	T	F	S
						1
2	3	4	5	6	7	8
9	10	11	12	13	14	15
16	17	18	19	20	21	22
23/30	24/31	25	26	27	28	29

JUNE

S	M	T	W	T	F	S
		1	2	3	4	5
6	7	8	9	10	11	12
13	14	15	16	17	18	19
20	21	22	23	24	25	26
27	28	29	30			

8
saturday

Mother's Day (U.S., Canada, Australia, N.Z.)

9
sunday

May

10
monday

Sri Yukteswar's Birthday

11
tuesday

New Moon ●

12^{20} Dr. Geeta VV

10 - Dr Lisa

12
wednesday

13
thursday 11^{15} alice

14
friday

15
saturday

16
sunday

MAY

S	M	T	W	T	F	S
						1
2	3	4	5	6	7	8
9	10	11	12	13	14	15
16	17	18	19	20	21	22
23/30	24/31	25	26	27	28	29

JUNE

S	M	T	W	T	F	S
		1	2	3	4	5
6	7	8	9	10	11	12
13	14	15	16	17	18	19
20	21	22	23	24	25	26
27	28	29	30			

Heavenly Father, may Thy kingdom of peace come on earth as it is in heaven, that we all be freed from divisive inharmonies and become perfect citizens, in body, mind, and soul, of Thy world.

—Paramahansa Yogananda

Clearing rain shower, Kauai, Hawaii   Photograph by Olof Carmel

The nature of Spirit is joy; and the nature of your soul is joy.

—Paramahansa Yogananda

Northern parula, Ohio   Photograph by Gary Meszaros/Science Source

May

9^{30} Dr Athens

17
monday

2^{30} Dr Athens

18
tuesday

19
wednesday

First Quarter ◐

2^{30} Dr Athens

20
thursday

21
friday

22
saturday

23
sunday

May

S	M	T	W	T	F	S
						1
2	3	4	5	6	7	8
9	10	11	12	13	14	15
16	17	18	19	20	21	22
23/30	24/31	25	26	27	28	29

June

S	M	T	W	T	F	S
		1	2	3	4	5
6	7	8	9	10	11	12
13	14	15	16	17	18	19
20	21	22	23	24	25	26
27	28	29	30			

May

24
monday

Victoria Day (Canada)

noon – Dr Ademola – weigh

25
tuesday

925-953-3952
Sreemanta

26
wednesday

Full Moon ○

10:30 – 11:30 HTGT

27
thursday

12:20 Mariana

28
friday

29
saturday

30
sunday

May

S	M	T	W	T	F	S
						1
2	3	4	5	6	7	8
9	10	11	12	13	14	15
16	17	18	19	20	21	22
23/30	24/31	25	26	27	28	29

June

S	M	T	W	T	F	S
		1	2	3	4	5
6	7	8	9	10	11	12
13	14	15	16	17	18	19
20	21	22	23	24	25	26
27	28	29	30			

The word *yoga* signifies the perfect poise or mental evenness that is the result of communion of the mind with Spirit.

—Paramahansa Yogananda

Swans, Japanese Tea Garden, Portland, Oregon   Photograph by Cindy Kassab/AKM Images

Purity, peace, happiness beyond dreams,
are sparkling and dancing within your soul.

—Paramahansa Yogananda

Proxy Falls, Three Sisters Wilderness, Oregon   Photograph by Chuck Haney/Danita Delimont Stock

May/June

Memorial Day

31
monday

1
tuesday

Last Quarter ◑

2
wednesday

11[15] Alice

3
thursday

4
friday

5
saturday

6
sunday

MAY

S	M	T	W	T	F	S
						1
2	3	4	5	6	7	8
9	10	11	12	13	14	15
16	17	18	19	20	21	22
23/30	24/31	25	26	27	28	29

JUNE

S	M	T	W	T	F	S
		1	2	3	4	5
6	7	8	9	10	11	12
13	14	15	16	17	18	19
20	21	22	23	24	25	26
27	28	29	30			

June

7
monday

8
tuesday

noon. Mit

9
wednesday

10
thursday

New Moon ●

11
friday

12
saturday

13
sunday

June

S	M	T	W	T	F	S
		1	2	3	4	5
6	7	8	9	10	11	12
13	14	15	16	17	18	19
20	21	22	23	24	25	26
27	28	29	30			

July

S	M	T	W	T	F	S
				1	2	3
4	5	6	7	8	9	10
11	12	13	14	15	16	17
18	19	20	21	22	23	24
25	26	27	28	29	30	31

We are here for only a little while,
and we must make the best of every moment in our life.

—Paramahansa Yogananda

Streamertail hummingbird, Jamaica Photograph by Glenn Bartley/Minden Pictures

Conscience is intuitive reasoning, reporting the truth about yourself and your motives. When your conscience is clear, when you know you are doing right, you are not afraid of anything.

—Paramahansa Yogananda

Rescued Bengal tiger, adult male Photograph by Dave Welling

June

11 - Lisa

14
monday

15
tuesday

2 - Emily
initial evaluation

16
wednesday

Aurora

First Quarter ◐

17
thursday

18
friday

JUNE

S	M	T	W	T	F	S
		1	2	3	4	5
6	7	8	9	10	11	12
13	14	15	16	17	18	19
20	21	22	23	24	25	26
27	28	29	30			

19
saturday

JULY

S	M	T	W	T	F	S
				1	2	3
4	5	6	7	8	9	10
11	12	13	14	15	16	17
18	19	20	21	22	23	24
25	26	27	28	29	30	31

Father's Day (U.S., Canada, U.K.) Summer Solstice

20
sunday

June

21
monday

International Day of Yoga

22
tuesday

11[45] - Emily

23
wednesday

1 - Alice

24
thursday

Full Moon ○

25
friday

26
saturday

27
sunday

JUNE

S	M	T	W	T	F	S
		1	2	3	4	5
6	7	8	9	10	11	12
13	14	15	16	17	18	19
20	21	22	23	24	25	26
27	28	29	30			

JULY

S	M	T	W	T	F	S
				1	2	3
4	5	6	7	8	9	10
11	12	13	14	15	16	17
18	19	20	21	22	23	24
25	26	27	28	29	30	31

When you are united with Spirit, you are king — a king of quietude and bliss, fully satisfied and complete within your Self.

—Paramahansa Yogananda

Val Di Funes, Italy   Photograph by Steve Guadarrama

Meditation is the pickax that pries up all the covers of consciousness, and brings forth the fountain of God's ever new joy.

—Paramahansa Yogananda

Fly geyser, Hualapai Flat, Nevada   Photograph by Frans Lanting

June/July

28
monday

29
tuesday

~~1^{45} - Emily~~

30
wednesday

10^{30} - 11^{15} HTGT

2 - Emily

Canada Day (Canada) Last Quarter ◑

1
thursday

noon - Mariana

2
friday

3
saturday

Independence Day

4
sunday

JUNE

S	M	T	W	T	F	S
		1	2	3	4	5
6	7	8	9	10	11	12
13	14	15	16	17	18	19
20	21	22	23	24	25	26
27	28	29	30			

JULY

S	M	T	W	T	F	S
				1	2	3
4	5	6	7	8	9	10
11	12	13	14	15	16	17
18	19	20	21	22	23	24
25	26	27	28	29	30	31

July

shower
estradial

5
monday

6
tuesday 11[45] - Emily

7
wednesday 11[45] Dr Ademola

hair color / shower
estradiol

8
thursday

AM white flower

9
friday

New Moon ●

10
saturday

shower
estradiol

11
sunday

JULY

S	M	T	W	T	F	S
				1	2	3
4	5	6	7	8	9	10
11	12	13	14	15	16	17
18	19	20	21	22	23	24
25	26	27	28	29	30	31

AUGUST

S	M	T	W	T	F	S
1	2	3	4	5	6	7
8	9	10	11	12	13	14
15	16	17	18	19	20	21
22	23	24	25	26	27	28
29	30	31				

The river of divine friendship broadens as it flows onward, powerful and truthful, eventually merging in the oceanic presence of God.

—Paramahansa Yogananda

Athabasca Falls, Jasper National Park, Alberta, Canada Photograph by Mike Grandmaison

*T*he purpose of this life is to find your Self. Know your Self.
Feel the throb of the ocean of God's presence in your heart.

—Paramahansa Yogananda

Bottle-nosed dolphins, Caribbean Sea   Photograph by F. Lukasseck/Masterfile

July

~~11 45 ...~~ Mril

12 monday

12 30 PT

13 tuesday

shower
estradiol

11- Jan

14 wednesday

11 15 Alice

15 thursday

12 40 Dr gaeta VV

16 friday

shower
estradiol

First Quarter ◐

17 saturday

18 sunday

July						
S	M	T	W	T	F	S
				1	2	3
4	5	6	7	8	9	10
11	12	13	14	15	16	17
18	19	20	21	22	23	24
25	26	27	28	29	30	31

August						
S	M	T	W	T	F	S
1	2	3	4	5	6	7
8	9	10	11	12	13	14
15	16	17	18	19	20	21
22	23	24	25	26	27	28
29	30	31				

July

19
monday

20
tuesday

21
wednesday

22
thursday

23
friday

Full Moon ○

24
saturday

25
sunday

Mahavatar Babaji Commemoration Day

July

S	M	T	W	T	F	S
				1	2	3
4	5	6	7	8	9	10
11	12	13	14	15	16	17
18	19	20	21	22	23	24
25	26	27	28	29	30	31

August

S	M	T	W	T	F	S
1	2	3	4	5	6	7
8	9	10	11	12	13	14
15	16	17	18	19	20	21
22	23	24	25	26	27	28
29	30	31				

All of God's expressions in nature send out a vibration
that in some way serves the world.

—Paramahansa Yogananda

Caracas Botanical Garden, Venezuela Photograph by E. E. Marys/AGE Fotostock

The divine lover beholds God through every window of thought and space, and the Cosmic Beloved beholds the devotee through every window of His omnipresent love.

—Paramahansa Yogananda

House finch, Bodie State Park, California Photograph by John Hendrickson

July/August

11 - Dr. Lisa

26
monday

~~11:45 - Emily~~ [illegible]

27
tuesday

Jan

28
wednesday

10:30 - 11:30, HTGT

12:30 - Aurora

29
thursday

30
friday

July

S	M	T	W	T	F	S
				1	2	3
4	5	6	7	8	9	10
11	12	13	14	15	16	17
18	19	20	21	22	23	24
25	26	27	28	29	30	31

August

S	M	T	W	T	F	S
1	2	3	4	5	6	7
8	9	10	11	12	13	14
15	16	17	18	19	20	21
22	23	24	25	26	27	28
29	30	31				

Last Quarter ◑

31
saturday

1
sunday

August

2
monday
~~11⁴⁵ Pinnacle~~

3
tuesday

12³⁰ Mariana

4
wednesday

5
thursday
~~11¹⁵ Alice~~

12

~~2¹⁵ annual physical~~
~~Dr Ademola~~

6
friday

7
saturday

8
sunday

New Moon ●

AUGUST

S	M	T	W	T	F	S
1	2	3	4	5	6	7
8	9	10	11	12	13	14
15	16	17	18	19	20	21
22	23	24	25	26	27	28
29	30	31				

SEPTEMBER

S	M	T	W	T	F	S
			1	2	3	4
5	6	7	8	9	10	11
12	13	14	15	16	17	18
19	20	21	22	23	24	25
26	27	28	29	30		

When the mind is calm, how quickly, how smoothly, how beautifully you will perceive everything!

—Paramahansa Yogananda

Mt. Shuksan and Picture Lake, Washington   Photograph by Tom Mackie

God wants His children to live simply and to be content with innocent pleasures.

—Paramahansa Yogananda

Baby koala bear, eastern Australia   Photograph by Gary Bell/Oceanwide Images

August

~~noon - Mait~~

9
monday

11:45 Pinnacle

10
tuesday

↑

11
wednesday

12:30 Alice

11 - Jan

12
thursday

13
friday

AUGUST

S	M	T	W	T	F	S
1	2	3	4	5	6	7
8	9	10	11	12	13	14
15	16	17	18	19	20	21
22	23	24	25	26	27	28
29	30	31				

SEPTEMBER

S	M	T	W	T	F	S
			1	2	3	4
5	6	7	8	9	10	11
12	13	14	15	16	17	18
19	20	21	22	23	24	25
26	27	28	29	30		

14
saturday

First Quarter ◐

15
sunday

noon - [illegible]

August

16
monday

17
tuesday
11^{45} Pinnacle

18
wednesday

19
thursday

1^{30} Dr Ademola
annual exam

20
friday

Patricia's
Party

21
saturday

22
sunday

Full Moon ○

AUGUST

S	M	T	W	T	F	S
1	2	3	4	5	6	7
8	9	10	11	12	13	14
15	16	17	18	19	20	21
22	23	24	25	26	27	28
29	30	31				

SEPTEMBER

S	M	T	W	T	F	S
			1	2	3	4
5	6	7	8	9	10	11
12	13	14	15	16	17	18
19	20	21	22	23	24	25
26	27	28	29	30		

The purpose of meditation is to calm the mind, that without distortion it may mirror Omnipresence.

—Paramahansa Yogananda

Ottawa River near Latulipe, Quebec   Photograph by Mike Grandmaison

Through the intuition of your soul feel the manifestation of God bursting through the clouds of your restlessness as great peace and joy.

—Paramahansa Yogananda

Double rainbow, Kauai, Hawaii Photograph by Elizabeth Carmel

August

11-Dr Lisa

23
monday

11^45 Niraj

24
tuesday

10-
11-Jan

25
wednesday

9^45-10^45 HTGT

26
thursday

27
friday

AUGUST

S	M	T	W	T	F	S
1	2	3	4	5	6	7
8	9	10	11	12	13	14
15	16	17	18	19	20	21
22	23	24	25	26	27	28
29	30	31				

28
saturday

SEPTEMBER

S	M	T	W	T	F	S
			1	2	3	4
5	6	7	8	9	10	11
12	13	14	15	16	17	18
19	20	21	22	23	24	25
26	27	28	29	30		

29
sunday

August/September

30
monday

3:00 Dr Athens
Optometry

Janmashtami Last Quarter ◑

31
tuesday

~~1:45 Nirot~~

1
wednesday

2
thursday

3:30 hearing test
Dr. Kinder

3
friday

~~1:20 Mariana~~

4
saturday

5
sunday

AUGUST

S	M	T	W	T	F	S
1	2	3	4	5	6	7
8	9	10	11	12	13	14
15	16	17	18	19	20	21
22	23	24	25	26	27	28
29	30	31				

SEPTEMBER

S	M	T	W	T	F	S
			1	2	3	4
5	6	7	8	9	10	11
12	13	14	15	16	17	18
19	20	21	22	23	24	25
26	27	28	29	30		

Remember only the beautiful things that you have felt, and seen, and experienced.
If your five senses behold only the good,
then your mind will be a garden of blossoming soul qualities.

—Paramahansa Yogananda

Mt. Revelstoke National Park, British Columbia, Canada Photograph by Michael Wheatley/All Canada Photos

When you try to experience your spiritual convictions, another world begins to open up to you.

—Paramahansa Yogananda

Mt. Baker Wilderness, Washington   Photograph by Michael Wheatley

September

6
monday

Labor Day (U.S. and Canada) Rosh Hashanah New Moon ●

11 30 Niraj

7
tuesday

8
wednesday

1- Aurora

9
thursday

1 30 Mariana

11 30 Alice

10
friday

SEPTEMBER

S	M	T	W	T	F	S
			1	2	3	4
5	6	7	8	9	10	11
12	13	14	15	16	17	18
19	20	21	22	23	24	25
26	27	28	29	30		

11
saturday

OCTOBER

S	M	T	W	T	F	S
					1	2
3	4	5	6	7	8	9
10	11	12	13	14	15	16
17	18	19	20	21	22	23
24/31	25	26	27	28	29	30

12
sunday

September

13
monday

First Quarter ◐

14
tuesday 11³⁰ Niraj

15
wednesday 2⁴⁰ Dr Sheik VV

Yom Kippur

16
thursday

17
friday

18
saturday

19
sunday

SEPTEMBER

S	M	T	W	T	F	S
			1	2	3	4
5	6	7	8	9	10	11
12	13	14	15	16	17	18
19	20	21	22	23	24	25
26	27	28	29	30		

OCTOBER

S	M	T	W	T	F	S
					1	2
3	4	5	6	7	8	9
10	11	12	13	14	15	16
17	18	19	20	21	22	23
24/31	25	26	27	28	29	30

In the stillness of my soul, come, Father, come! Possess me and make me feel, in and around me, Thine immortal presence.

—Paramahansa Yogananda

Lake at dawn, Scottish Highlands, U.K.   Photograph by Pete Cairns/Science Source

Talk to God every second of your life....He who is playing hide-and-seek in the beauty of the flowers, in souls, in noble passions, in dreams, shall come forth.

—Paramahansa Yogananda

North American raccoon, Minnesota Photograph by Don Johnston/All Canada Photos

September

Full Moon ○ — 20 monday

U.N. International Day of Peace — 21 tuesday

Autumnal Equinox — 22 wednesday

9⁴⁵-10⁴⁵ HTGT

23 thursday

24 friday

25 saturday

Lahiri Mahasaya's Mahasamadhi — 26 sunday

September

S	M	T	W	T	F	S
			1	2	3	4
5	6	7	8	9	10	11
12	13	14	15	16	17	18
19	20	21	22	23	24	25
26	27	28	29	30		

October

S	M	T	W	T	F	S
					1	2
3	4	5	6	7	8	9
10	11	12	13	14	15	16
17	18	19	20	21	22	23
24/31	25	26	27	28	29	30

September/October

27
monday
11 - Dr Lisa
4 - Dr Ragurkus

28
tuesday
Last Quarter ◑

29
wednesday
11:45 mri
2:45 Andrea Adriane (Dr Tseng)

30
thursday
11:00 Bone Scan
no nuts or CA
x 24 hrs
Lahiri Mahasaya's Birthday

1
friday

2
saturday

3
sunday
10-10:30
HTGT

September

S	M	T	W	T	F	S
			1	2	3	4
5	6	7	8	9	10	11
12	13	14	15	16	17	18
19	20	21	22	23	24	25
26	27	28	29	30		

October

S	M	T	W	T	F	S
					1	2
3	4	5	6	7	8	9
10	11	12	13	14	15	16
17	18	19	20	21	22	23
24/31	25	26	27	28	29	30

Every noble thought in your mind brings you closer to God. Those thoughts are like a river leading to the ocean of Spirit.

—Paramahansa Yogananda

Magalloway River, Maine   Photograph by Paul Rezendes

Wherever you go, conduct yourself with the consciousness that you are the master of yourself.

—Paramahansa Yogananda

Brown bear, Finland Photograph by Danny Green/Nature Picture Library

October

4
monday

5
tuesday

New Moon ●

6
wednesday

11³⁰ Alice

7
thursday

Washing machine

8
friday

October

S	M	T	W	T	F	S
					1	2
3	4	5	6	7	8	9
10	11	12	13	14	15	16
17	18	19	20	21	22	23
24/31	25	26	27	28	29	30

9
saturday

November

S	M	T	W	T	F	S
	1	2	3	4	5	6
7	8	9	10	11	12	13
14	15	16	17	18	19	20
21	22	23	24	25	26	27
28	29	30				

10
sunday

October

11
monday

Columbus Day/Indigenous Peoples' Day   Thanksgiving Day (Canada)

12
tuesday

First Quarter ◐

13
wednesday

14
thursday

15
friday

16
saturday

10 - Scott

17
sunday

October

S	M	T	W	T	F	S
					1	2
3	4	5	6	7	8	9
10	11	12	13	14	15	16
17	18	19	20	21	22	23
24/31	25	26	27	28	29	30

November

S	M	T	W	T	F	S
	1	2	3	4	5	6
7	8	9	10	11	12	13
14	15	16	17	18	19	20
21	22	23	24	25	26	27
28	29	30				

We exist, and that existence is eternal....This body has come, and it will vanish; but the soul essence within it will never cease to exist. Nothing can terminate that eternal consciousness.

—Paramahansa Yogananda

Kilauea volcano and Milky Way, Hawaii   Photograph by Gary Hart

If we can learn to understand others, and to free our minds from all prejudices born of environment, we begin to express the perfect image of God within us and to find it in all.

—Paramahansa Yogananda

Etosha National Park, Namibia   Photograph by Art Wolfe

October

18
monday

19
tuesday

Full Moon ○

20
wednesday

2 - Aurora

21
thursday

456-5776
2 - Karen

22
friday

OCTOBER

S	M	T	W	T	F	S
					1	2
3	4	5	6	7	8	9
10	11	12	13	14	15	16
17	18	19	20	21	22	23
24/31	25	26	27	28	29	30

NOVEMBER

S	M	T	W	T	F	S
	1	2	3	4	5	6
7	8	9	10	11	12	13
14	15	16	17	18	19	20
21	22	23	24	25	26	27
28	29	30				

23
saturday

24
sunday

October

25
monday

26 11- Dr Lisa 2 - Preeta
tuesday

27 2- Dr Tseng ↓
wednesday

28 10 15 HTGT Amit - 11 45
thursday
Last Quarter ◑

29
friday

30
saturday

31
sunday
Daylight Saving Time ends (U.K. and European Union)
Halloween (U.S., Canada, U.K.)

October

S	M	T	W	T	F	S
					1	2
3	4	5	6	7	8	9
10	11	12	13	14	15	16
17	18	19	20	21	22	23
24/31	25	26	27	28	29	30

November

S	M	T	W	T	F	S
	1	2	3	4	5	6
7	8	9	10	11	12	13
14	15	16	17	18	19	20
21	22	23	24	25	26	27
28	29	30				

Your

2022 Inner Reflections Engagement Calendar

is now available online and in select bookstores

You may also place your order directly from Self-Realization Fellowship by calling 818-549-5151 Monday – Friday from 9:00 a.m. to 5:00 p.m. Pacific time or order online at:
www.srfbooks.org

If you would like a free copy of Self-Realization Fellowship's complete catalog of books and recordings, please call the number above or fill out the form below and mail to:

Self-Realization Fellowship
3880 San Rafael Ave.
Los Angeles, CA 90065-3219 U.S.A.
www.yogananda.org

Name: ______________________________

Address: ______________________________

City: ____________________ State: _____ Zip code: __________

Country: ______________________________

Everything that is visible is the result of the Invisible. Because you do not see God, you do not believe He is here. Yet every tree and every blade of grass is controlled by the power of God within it.

—Paramahansa Yogananda

Tundra with black spruce, Denali National Park, Alaska   Photograph by Olof Carmel

Feel the love of God....You will find a magic, living relationship uniting the trees, the sky, the stars, all people, and all living things; and you will feel a oneness with them. This is the code of divine love.

—Paramahansa Yogananda

Aurora Borealis over Sycamore Gap, Northumberland, U.K. Photograph by Guy Edwardes/Nature Picture Library

November

1
monday

General Election Day

2
tuesday

3
wednesday

11^{30}

New Moon ●

4
thursday

5
friday

NOVEMBER

S	M	T	W	T	F	S
	1	2	3	4	5	6
7	8	9	10	11	12	13
14	15	16	17	18	19	20
21	22	23	24	25	26	27
28	29	30				

DECEMBER

S	M	T	W	T	F	S
			1	2	3	4
5	6	7	8	9	10	11
12	13	14	15	16	17	18
19	20	21	22	23	24	25
26	27	28	29	30	31	

6
saturday

Daylight Saving Time ends (U.S. and Canada)

7
sunday

November

8
monday

9
tuesday

10
wednesday

11
thursday

11-COVID Booster Safeway

Veterans Day Remembrance Day (Canada) First Quarter ◐

12
friday

~~10-1830 HFGT~~

12:20 Dr Gaeta Facetime

13
saturday

14
sunday

Remembrance Sunday (U.K.)

November

S	M	T	W	T	F	S
	1	2	3	4	5	6
7	8	9	10	11	12	13
14	15	16	17	18	19	20
21	22	23	24	25	26	27
28	29	30				

December

S	M	T	W	T	F	S
			1	2	3	4
5	6	7	8	9	10	11
12	13	14	15	16	17	18
19	20	21	22	23	24	25
26	27	28	29	30	31	

You are on a journey, stopping here for just a little while.
Life is like a great caravan passing by.
Your first interest should be to learn the purpose of this journey,
and its destination. That destination is God.

—Paramahansa Yogananda

Tundra valley, Alaska Photograph by Frans Lanting

One secret of progress is self-analysis. Introspection is a mirror in which to see recesses of your mind that otherwise would remain hidden from you.

—Paramahansa Yogananda

Lake Jasna, Slovenia   Photograph by Tom Mackie

November

15
monday

16
tuesday

17
wednesday

18
thursday

Full Moon ○

19
friday

NOVEMBER

S	M	T	W	T	F	S
	1	2	3	4	5	6
7	8	9	10	11	12	13
14	15	16	17	18	19	20
21	22	23	24	25	26	27
28	29	30				

DECEMBER

S	M	T	W	T	F	S
			1	2	3	4
5	6	7	8	9	10	11
12	13	14	15	16	17	18
19	20	21	22	23	24	25
26	27	28	29	30	31	

20
saturday

21
sunday

November

22
monday
11-Dr. Lisa

23
tuesday

10-HTGT

24
wednesday

25
thursday
Thanksgiving Day

26
friday

27
saturday
Last Quarter ◑

28
sunday
Hanukkah

NOVEMBER

S	M	T	W	T	F	S
	1	2	3	4	5	6
7	8	9	10	11	12	13
14	15	16	17	18	19	20
21	22	23	24	25	26	27
28	29	30				

DECEMBER

S	M	T	W	T	F	S
			1	2	3	4
5	6	7	8	9	10	11
12	13	14	15	16	17	18
19	20	21	22	23	24	25
26	27	28	29	30	31	

Divine Abundance follows the law of service and generosity. Give and then receive. Give to the world the best you have and the best will come back to you.

—Paramahansa Yogananda

Glade Creek, Babcock State Park, West Virginia   Photograph by Mike Briner/AKM Images

Divine Joy outlasts everything. It is enduring.
When all else melts away, that Joy remains.

—Paramahansa Yogananda

Mt. Herzogstand, Bavaria, Germany   Photograph by Wilfried Bahnm/AGE Fotostock

November/December

29
monday

30
tuesday

1
wednesday

11[30] Alice massage

3[30] Aurora

2
thursday

3
friday

New Moon ●

4
saturday

5
sunday

NOVEMBER

S	M	T	W	T	F	S
	1	2	3	4	5	6
7	8	9	10	11	12	13
14	15	16	17	18	19	20
21	22	23	24	25	26	27
28	29	30				

DECEMBER

S	M	T	W	T	F	S
			1	2	3	4
5	6	7	8	9	10	11
12	13	14	15	16	17	18
19	20	21	22	23	24	25
26	27	28	29	30	31	

December

12^{30} shingles #2
Safeway

6
monday

7
tuesday

8
wednesday

Mari + 11^{45}

12^{30} Maria

$10\ 10^{30}$ HTGT

9
thursday

10
friday

First Quarter ◐

11
saturday

12
sunday

DECEMBER

S	M	T	W	T	F	S
			1	2	3	4
5	6	7	8	9	10	11
12	13	14	15	16	17	18
19	20	21	22	23	24	25
26	27	28	29	30	31	

JANUARY 2022

S	M	T	W	T	F	S
						1
2	3	4	5	6	7	8
9	10	11	12	13	14	15
16	17	18	19	20	21	22
23/30	24/31	25	26	27	28	29

The joyous rays of the soul may be perceived if you interiorize your attention.... In the airplane of your visualization, glide over the limitless empire of thoughts. There behold the mountain ranges of unbroken, lofty, spiritual aspirations for improving yourself and others.

—Paramahansa Yogananda

Northern lights over Lofoten Islands, Norway Photograph by Roberto Moiola/First Light

Thoughts are rivers flowing from the reservoir of Spirit. To connect your life with Spirit is the most important duty.

—Paramahansa Yogananda

Truckee River, Northern California   Photograph by Tom Mackie

December

13
monday

14
tuesday

15
wednesday

16
thursday

17
friday

December

S	M	T	W	T	F	S
			1	2	3	4
5	6	7	8	9	10	11
12	13	14	15	16	17	18
19	20	21	22	23	24	25
26	27	28	29	30	31	

Full Moon ○

18
saturday

January 2022

S	M	T	W	T	F	S
						1
2	3	4	5	6	7	8
9	10	11	12	13	14	15
16	17	18	19	20	21	22
23/30	24/31	25	26	27	28	29

2-4 Karen's tea

19
sunday

December

20
monday
11-Dr Lisa

21
tuesday
Winter Solstice

22
wednesday

23
thursday

24
friday
10-HTGT

25
saturday
Christmas

26
sunday
Boxing Day (Canada, U.K., Australia, N.Z.) Last Quarter ◑

December

S	M	T	W	T	F	S
			1	2	3	4
5	6	7	8	9	10	11
12	13	14	15	16	17	18
19	20	21	22	23	24	25
26	27	28	29	30	31	

January 2022

S	M	T	W	T	F	S
						1
2	3	4	5	6	7	8
9	10	11	12	13	14	15
16	17	18	19	20	21	22
23/30	24/31	25	26	27	28	29

Celebrate the birth of Christ in the cradle of your consciousness during the Christmas season. Let His vast perception in Nature, in space, and in universal love be felt within your heart.

—Paramahansa Yogananda

Northern cardinal, near Marion, Illinois   Photograph by Richard & Susan Day/Danita Delimont Stock

When you use life's experiences as your teacher,
and learn from them the true nature of the world and your part in it,
those experiences become valuable guides to eternal fulfillment and happiness.

—Paramahansa Yogananda

Sunset, Lake Tahoe, Nevada   Photograph by Elizabeth Carmel

December/January

27
monday

28
tuesday

29
wednesday

11:20 Alice massage

30
thursday

31
friday

New Year's Day

1
saturday

New Moon ●

2
sunday

DECEMBER

S	M	T	W	T	F	S
			1	2	3	4
5	6	7	8	9	10	11
12	13	14	15	16	17	18
19	20	21	22	23	24	25
26	27	28	29	30	31	

JANUARY 2022

S	M	T	W	T	F	S
						1
2	3	4	5	6	7	8
9	10	11	12	13	14	15
16	17	18	19	20	21	22
23/30	24/31	25	26	27	28	29

NOTES

✍

ACKNOWLEDGMENTS

We wish to express our sincere appreciation to the following photographers and agencies who contributed to this year's *Inner Reflections* engagement calendar. Following a contributor's name, in parentheses, is the month and a day of the week, or other description, where each photo appears.

Accent Alaska (3/29)
AGE Fotostock (4/19, 7/19, 11/29)
AKM Images (5/24, 11/22)
All Canada Photos (8/30, 9/20)
Mary Liz Austin (1/18)
Wilfried Bahnm/AGE Fotostock (11/29)
Glenn Bartley/Minden Pictures (6/7)
Gary Bell/Oceanwide Images (1/11, 8/9)
Mike Briner/AKM Images (11/22)
Russ Burden (1/25)
Pete Cairns/Science Source (9/13)
Elizabeth Carmel (8/23, 12/27)
Olof Carmel (5/10, 10/25)
Danita Delimont Stock (5/31, 12/20)
Richard & Susan Day (3/1)
Richard & Susan Day/Danita Delimont (12/20)
Donna Dewhurst/Accent Alaska (3/29)
Guy Edwardes/Nature Picture Library (11/1)
First Light (2/15, 12/6)
Tim Fitzharris (2/22)
Andre & Anita Gilden/First Light (2/15)
Mike Grandmaison (3/22, 7/5, 8/16)
Danny Green/Nature Picture Library (10/4)
Steve Guadarrama (6/21)
Darrell Gulin (3/15, 5/3)
Chuck Haney/Danita Delimont Stock (5/31)
Gary Hart (3/8, 10/11)
John Hendrickson (7/26)
Don Johnston (Front Cover)
Don Johnston/All Canada Photos (9/20)
Cindy Kassab/AKM Images (5/24)
Lewis Kemper (1/4)
Frans Lanting (6/28, 11/8)
Raimond Linke/Masterfile (4/5)
F. Lukasseck/Masterfile (7/12)
Tom Mackie (8/2, 11/15, 12/13)
E. E. Marys/AGE Fotostock (7/19)
Masterfile (12/28/20, 4/5, 4/26, 7/12)
B. Mauritius/AGE Fotostock (4/19)
Gary Meszaros/Science Source (5/17)
Minden Pictures (6/7)
Roberto Moiola/First Light (12/6)
Nature Picture Library (10/4, 11/1)
Oceanwide Images (1/11, 8/9)
Londie G. Padelsky (4/12)
Don Paulson (2/8)
Aflo Relax/Masterfile (4/26)
Paul Rezendes (2/1, 9/27)
Martin Ruegner/Masterfile (12/28/20)
Science Source (5/17, 9/13)
Dave Welling (6/14)
Michael Wheatley/All Canada Photos (8/30)
Michael Wheatley (9/6)
Art Wolfe (10/18)

About Paramahansa Yogananda

Paramahansa Yogananda
1893-1952

All the quotes featured in *Inner Reflections* have been selected from the writings of Paramahansa Yogananda, one of the preeminent spiritual teachers of the 20th century. Yogananda came to the United States in 1920 as India's delegate to an international congress of religious leaders convening in Boston. He remained in the West for the better part of the next thirty-two years, conducting classes in cities across America, counseling, and creating a monumental body of written work.

Paramahansa Yogananda's life story, *Autobiography of a Yogi,* is considered a modern spiritual classic. It was selected one of "The Top 100 Spiritual Books of the Twentieth Century" in a survey conducted by HarperCollins. A perennial best seller since it was first published in 1946, *Autobiography of a Yogi* has been translated into more than fifty languages and is widely used in college and university courses.

An award-winning documentary film about Paramahansa Yogananda's life and work, *Awake: The Life of Yogananda,* was released in October 2014.

For more information about SRF publications and the teachings of Paramahansa Yogananda, please visit our website:

www.yogananda.org

Self-Realization Fellowship
FOUNDED 1920 BY PARAMAHANSA YOGANANDA

The year 2020 marked the 100th anniversary of Self-Realization Fellowship, the international nonprofit society Paramahansa Yogananda founded to oversee the worldwide dissemination of his teachings. Self-Realization Fellowship is dedicated to carrying on his spiritual and humanitarian work — fostering a spirit of greater harmony and understanding among those of all nations and faiths, and introducing truth-seekers around the world to his universal teachings on the ancient science of yoga.

A SELECTION OF BOOKS BY PARAMAHANSA YOGANANDA

Available at bookstores or from our website:
www.srfbooks.org

Autobiography of a Yogi

Autobiography of a Yogi *(Audiobook, read by Sir Ben Kingsley)*

The Science of Religion

The Law of Success

How You Can Talk With God

Metaphysical Meditations

Where There Is Light: *Insight and Inspiration for Meeting Life's Challenges*

The Yoga of Jesus: *Understanding the Hidden Teachings of the Gospels*

The Yoga of the Bhagavad Gita: *An Introduction to India's Universal Science of God-Realization*

The Collected Talks and Essays
Volume I: Man's Eternal Quest
Volume II: The Divine Romance
Volume III: Journey to Self-realization

DVD VIDEO

Awake: The Life of Yogananda
A film by CounterPoint Films

SELF-REALIZATION FELLOWSHIP LESSONS

The scientific techniques of meditation taught by Paramahansa Yogananda, including Kriya Yoga — as well as his guidance on all aspects of balanced spiritual living — are taught in the *Self-Realization Fellowship Lessons*. For more information please visit www.srflessons.org.

SELF-REALIZATION FELLOWSHIP

3880 San Rafael Avenue • Los Angeles, CA 90065-3219

TEL (323) 225-2471 • FAX (323) 225-5088

www.yogananda.org

2020

January

s	m	t	w	t	f	s
			1	2	3	4
5	6	7	8	9	10	11
12	13	14	15	16	17	18
19	20	21	22	23	24	25
26	27	28	29	30	31	

February

s	m	t	w	t	f	s
						1
2	3	4	5	6	7	8
9	10	11	12	13	14	15
16	17	18	19	20	21	22
23	24	25	26	27	28	29

March

s	m	t	w	t	f	s
1	2	3	4	5	6	7
8	9	10	11	12	13	14
15	16	17	18	19	20	21
22	23	24	25	26	27	28
29	30	31				

April

s	m	t	w	t	f	s
			1	2	3	4
5	6	7	8	9	10	11
12	13	14	15	16	17	18
19	20	21	22	23	24	25
26	27	28	29	30		

May

s	m	t	w	t	f	s
					1	2
3	4	5	6	7	8	9
10	11	12	13	14	15	16
17	18	19	20	21	22	23
24/31	25	26	27	28	29	30

June

s	m	t	w	t	f	s
	1	2	3	4	5	6
7	8	9	10	11	12	13
14	15	16	17	18	19	20
21	22	23	24	25	26	27
28	29	30				

July

s	m	t	w	t	f	s
			1	2	3	4
5	6	7	8	9	10	11
12	13	14	15	16	17	18
19	20	21	22	23	24	25
26	27	28	29	30	31	

August

s	m	t	w	t	f	s
						1
2	3	4	5	6	7	8
9	10	11	12	13	14	15
16	17	18	19	20	21	22
23/30	24/31	25	26	27	28	29

September

s	m	t	w	t	f	s
		1	2	3	4	5
6	7	8	9	10	11	12
13	14	15	16	17	18	19
20	21	22	23	24	25	26
27	28	29	30			

October

s	m	t	w	t	f	s
				1	2	3
4	5	6	7	8	9	10
11	12	13	14	15	16	17
18	19	20	21	22	23	24
25	26	27	28	29	30	31

November

s	m	t	w	t	f	s
1	2	3	4	5	6	7
8	9	10	11	12	13	14
15	16	17	18	19	20	21
22	23	24	25	26	27	28
29	30					

December

s	m	t	w	t	f	s
		1	2	3	4	5
6	7	8	9	10	11	12
13	14	15	16	17	18	19
20	21	22	23	24	25	26
27	28	29	30	31		

2022

January

s	m	t	w	t	f	s
						1
2	3	4	5	6	7	8
9	10	11	12	13	14	15
16	17	18	19	20	21	22
23/30	24/31	25	26	27	28	29

February

s	m	t	w	t	f	s
		1	2	3	4	5
6	7	8	9	10	11	12
13	14	15	16	17	18	19
20	21	22	23	24	25	26
27	28					

March

s	m	t	w	t	f	s
		1	2	3	4	5
6	7	8	9	10	11	12
13	14	15	16	17	18	19
20	21	22	23	24	25	26
27	28	29	30	31		

April

s	m	t	w	t	f	s
					1	2
3	4	5	6	7	8	9
10	11	12	13	14	15	16
17	18	19	20	21	22	23
24	25	26	27	28	29	30

May

s	m	t	w	t	f	s
1	2	3	4	5	6	7
8	9	10	11	12	13	14
15	16	17	18	19	20	21
22	23	24	25	26	27	28
29	30	31				

June

s	m	t	w	t	f	s
			1	2	3	4
5	6	7	8	9	10	11
12	13	14	15	16	17	18
19	20	21	22	23	24	25
26	27	28	29	30		

July

s	m	t	w	t	f	s
					1	2
3	4	5	6	7	8	9
10	11	12	13	14	15	16
17	18	19	20	21	22	23
24/31	25	26	27	28	29	30

August

s	m	t	w	t	f	s
	1	2	3	4	5	6
7	8	9	10	11	12	13
14	15	16	17	18	19	20
21	22	23	24	25	26	27
28	29	30	31			

September

s	m	t	w	t	f	s
				1	2	3
4	5	6	7	8	9	10
11	12	13	14	15	16	17
18	19	20	21	22	23	24
25	26	27	28	29	30	

October

s	m	t	w	t	f	s
						1
2	3	4	5	6	7	8
9	10	11	12	13	14	15
16	17	18	19	20	21	22
23/30	24/31	25	26	27	28	29

November

s	m	t	w	t	f	s
		1	2	3	4	5
6	7	8	9	10	11	12
13	14	15	16	17	18	19
20	21	22	23	24	25	26
27	28	29	30			

December

s	m	t	w	t	f	s
				1	2	3
4	5	6	7	8	9	10
11	12	13	14	15	16	17
18	19	20	21	22	23	24
25	26	27	28	29	30	31

2021

January

s	m	t	w	t	f	s
					1	2
3	4	5	6	7	8	9
10	11	12	13	14	15	16
17	18	19	20	21	22	23
24/31	25	26	27	28	29	30

February

s	m	t	w	t	f	s
	1	2	3	4	5	6
7	8	9	10	11	12	13
14	15	16	17	18	19	20
21	22	23	24	25	26	27
28						

March

s	m	t	w	t	f	s
	1	2	3	4	5	6
7	8	9	10	11	12	13
14	15	16	17	18	19	20
21	22	23	24	25	26	27
28	29	30	31			

April

s	m	t	w	t	f	s
				1	2	3
4	5	6	7	8	9	10
11	12	13	14	15	16	17
18	19	20	21	22	23	24
25	26	27	28	29	30	

May

s	m	t	w	t	f	s
						1
2	3	4	5	6	7	8
9	10	11	12	13	14	15
16	17	18	19	20	21	22
23/30	24/31	25	26	27	28	29

June

s	m	t	w	t	f	s
		1	2	3	4	5
6	7	8	9	10	11	12
13	14	15	16	17	18	19
20	21	22	23	24	25	26
27	28	29	30			

July

s	m	t	w	t	f	s
				1	2	3
4	5	6	7	8	9	10
11	12	13	14	15	16	17
18	19	20	21	22	23	24
25	26	27	28	29	30	31

August

s	m	t	w	t	f	s
1	2	3	4	5	6	7
8	9	10	11	12	13	14
15	16	17	18	19	20	21
22	23	24	25	26	27	28
29	30	31				

September

s	m	t	w	t	f	s
			1	2	3	4
5	6	7	8	9	10	11
12	13	14	15	16	17	18
19	20	21	22	23	24	25
26	27	28	29	30		

October

s	m	t	w	t	f	s
					1	2
3	4	5	6	7	8	9
10	11	12	13	14	15	16
17	18	19	20	21	22	23
24/31	25	26	27	28	29	30

November

s	m	t	w	t	f	s
	1	2	3	4	5	6
7	8	9	10	11	12	13
14	15	16	17	18	19	20
21	22	23	24	25	26	27
28	29	30				

December

s	m	t	w	t	f	s
			1	2	3	4
5	6	7	8	9	10	11
12	13	14	15	16	17	18
19	20	21	22	23	24	25
26	27	28	29	30	31	

January

Sunday	Monday	Tuesday	Wednesday	Thursday	Friday	Saturday
					1	2
3	4	5	6	7	8	9
10	11	12	13	14	15	16
17	18	19	20	21	22	23
24	25	26	27	28	29	30
31						

Jan. 1 New Year's Day
Jan. 5 Paramahansa Yogananda's Birthday
Jan. 18 Martin Luther King, Jr.'s Birthday (Observed)
Jan. 26 Australia Day (Australia)

FEBRUARY

Sunday	Monday	Tuesday	Wednesday	Thursday	Friday	Saturday
	1	2	3	4	5	6
7	8	9	10	11	12	13
14	15	16	17	18	19	20
21	22	23	24	25	26	27
28						

Feb. 14 St. Valentine's Day
Feb. 15 Presidents' Day

March

Sunday	Monday	Tuesday	Wednesday	Thursday	Friday	Saturday
	1	2	3	4	5	6
7	8	9	10	11	12	13
14	15	16	17	18	19	20
21	22	23	24	25	26	27
28	29	30	31			

March 7 Paramahansa Yogananda's Mahasamadhi
March 9 Sri Yukteswar's Mahasamadhi
March 14 Daylight Saving Time begins (U.S. and Canada)
March 17 St. Patrick's Day
March 20 Vernal Equinox
March 27 Passover begins
March 28 Daylight Savings Time begins (U.K. and European Union)

April

Sunday	Monday	Tuesday	Wednesday	Thursday	Friday	Saturday
				1	2	3
4	5	6	7	8	9	10
11	12	13	14	15	16	17
18	19	20	21	22	23	24
25	26	27	28	29	30	

April 2 Good Friday
April 4 Easter Sunday
April 5 Easter Monday (All except U.S. and Scotland)
April 22 Earth Day

May

Sunday	Monday	Tuesday	Wednesday	Thursday	Friday	Saturday
						1
2	3	4	5	6	7	8
9	10	11	12	13	14	15
16	17	18	19	20	21	22
23	24	25	26	27	28	29
30	31					

May 6 National Day of Prayer
May 9 Mother's Day (U.S., Canada, Australia, N.Z.)
May 10 Sri Yukteswar's Birthday
May 24 Victoria Day (Canada)
May 31 Memorial Day

June

Sunday	Monday	Tuesday	Wednesday	Thursday	Friday	Saturday
		1	2	3	4	5
6	7	8	9	10	11	12
13	14	15	16	17	18	19
20	21	22	23	24	25	26
27	28	29	30			

June 20 Father's Day (U.S., Canada, U.K.)
Summer Solstice
June 21 International Day of Yoga

July

Sunday	Monday	Tuesday	Wednesday	Thursday	Friday	Saturday
				1	2	3
4	5	6	7	8	9	10
11	12	13	14	15	16	17
18	19	20	21	22	23	24
25	26	27	28	29	30	31

July 1 Canada Day (Canada)
July 4 Independence Day
July 25 Mahavatar Babaji Commemoration Day

August

Sunday	Monday	Tuesday	Wednesday	Thursday	Friday	Saturday
1	2	3	4	5	6	7
8	9	10	11	12	13	14
15	16	17	18	19	20	21
22	23	24	25	26	27	28
29	30	31				

Aug. 30 Janmashtami

September

Sunday	Monday	Tuesday	Wednesday	Thursday	Friday	Saturday
			1	2	3	4
5	6	7	8	9	10	11
12	13	14	15	16	17	18
19	20	21	22	23	24	25
26	27	28	29	30		

Sept. 6 Labor Day (U.S. and Canada)
Rosh Hashanah
Sept. 15 Yom Kippur
Sept. 21 U.N. International Day of Peace
Sept. 22 Autumnal Equinox
Sept. 26 Lahiri Mahasaya's Mahasamadhi
Sept. 30 Lahiri Mahasaya's Birthday

October

Sunday	Monday	Tuesday	Wednesday	Thursday	Friday	Saturday
					1	2
3	4	5	6	7	8	9
10	11	12	13	14	15	16
17	18	19	20	21	22	23
24	25	26	27	28	29	30
31						

Oct. 11 Columbus Day/Indigenous Peoples' Day
Thanksgiving Day (Canada)

Oct. 31 Daylight Saving Time ends (European Union)
Halloween (U.S., Canada, U.K.)

November

Sunday	Monday	Tuesday	Wednesday	Thursday	Friday	Saturday
	1	2	3	4	5	6
7	8	9	10	11	12	13
14	15	16	17	18	19	20
21	22	23	24	25	26	27
28	29	30				

Nov. 2 General Election Day

Nov. 7 Daylight Saving Time ends (U.S. and Canada)

Nov. 11 Veterans Day
Remembrance Day (Canada)

Nov. 14 Remembrance Sunday (U.K.)

Nov. 25 Thanksgiving Day

Nov. 28 Hanukkah

December

Sunday	Monday	Tuesday	Wednesday	Thursday	Friday	Saturday
			1	2	3	4
5	6	7	8	9	10	11
12	13	14	15	16	17	18
19	20	21	22	23	24	25
26	27	28	29	30	31	

Dec. 21 Winter Solstice
Dec. 25 Christmas
Dec. 26 Boxing Day (Canada, U.K., Australia, N.Z.)

NOTES